New York

Photographs by Jon Ortner

A BOOK OF POSTCARDS

Impact, El Dorado Hills, CA

Over 25 million tourists visit New York City every year to experience the many attractions that almost eight million residents enjoy every day, including the Chrysler and Empire State Buildings and the World Trade Center–some of the tallest and most distinctive skyscrapers ever built.

Large and majestic suspension bridges such as the Brooklyn, George Washington, and Verrazano Narrows connect NYC's five boroughs, since Manhattan, Brooklyn/Queens, and Staten Island are separated from the mainland. Only the Bronx is part of the mainland.

World famous attractions such as the United Nations, Ellis Island, the South Street Seaport, and, of course, the Statue of Liberty are located throughout the city, as are the world class art collections of the Metropolitan, Modern Art, Guggenheim, Whitney, and Brooklyn Museums. No account of NY would be complete without mention of the performing arts; virtually every type of dance, music, and theater can be found here. Who hasn't heard of Broadway!

New York, a city of immigrants and refugees for three centuries, also has ethnic neighborhoods, each with its own language, restaurants, and traditions. Two of the most famous are Chinatown and Little Italy. Continue to enjoy the beauty and excitement of New York City after you return home with this book of postcards, or mail them and let your friends and relatives share your New York experience.

NEW YORK The sun sets over the southern tip of Manhattan and the Hudson River, with the Empire State Building at the heart of the city.

use
letter
rate

THIS AREA FOR OFFICIAL POSTAL USE ONLY

Photographs by
JON ORTNER

A dramatic twilight view of mid-town Manhattan. Clearly visible are the Citicorp, Met Life, and Chrysler Buildings.

use
letter
rate

THIS AREA FOR OFFICIAL POSTAL USE ONLY

Photographs by
JON ORTNER

The Statue of Liberty stands 306.8 feet above the New York harbor.

use
letter
rate

THIS AREA FOR OFFICIAL POSTAL USE ONLY

Photographs by
JON ORTNER

10

The New York Stock Exchange Trading Floor in a flurry of activity.

use
letter
rate

#43644 © Impact

THIS AREA FOR OFFICIAL POSTAL USE ONLY

Photographs by
JON ORTNER

NEW YORK

Glittering lights of New York City's West Side are reflected in the water of the Hudson River.

use letter rate

THIS AREA FOR OFFICIAL POSTAL USE ONLY

Photographs by
JON ORTNER

NEW YORK

The historic South Street Seaport, features restored ships and is a busy dining and shopping district on the East River.

use
letter
rate

THIS AREA FOR OFFICIAL POSTAL USE ONLY

Photographs by
JON ORTNER

GREEK GOLD
JEWELRY OF THE CLASSICAL WORLD
HANS COPER
R.B. Kitaj
A Retrospective

The Metropolitan Museum of Art
is the largest and most important
art museum in New York.

use
letter
rate

THIS AREA FOR OFFICIAL POSTAL USE ONLY

Photographs by
JON ORTNER

Rockefeller Center's Channel Garden is extravagantly decorated to reflect the holiday season.

use
letter
rate

THIS AREA FOR OFFICIAL POSTAL USE ONLY

Photographs by
JON ORTNER

NEW YORK

The Guggenheim Museum, located on Fifth Avenue, was designed by America's best-known architect, Frank Lloyd Wright.

use letter rate

THIS AREA FOR OFFICIAL POSTAL USE ONLY

Photographs by
JON ORTNER

NEW YORK

Located on the East River, the United Nations is comprised of the 39-story Secretarial Building, the General Assembly Building, the Conference Building, and the Dag Hammarskjold Library.

use
letter
rate

THIS AREA FOR OFFICIAL POSTAL USE ONLY

Photographs by
JON ORTNER

THEATRE
A NEW CHOICE IN PHONE, CABLE &
ERNET SERVICE 1-800-RING-SANTA
COMPUTERS CAMERAS
Collection

NEW YORK

Times Square and the Theater District are meccas for entertainment, dining and shopping.

use
letter
rate

THIS AREA FOR OFFICIAL POSTAL USE ONLY

Photographs by
JON ORTNER

The granite towers of the Brooklyn Bridge are strung with miles of steel suspension cables.

use
letter
rate

THIS AREA FOR OFFICIAL POSTAL USE ONLY

Photographs by
JON ORTNER

NEW YORK

Sunrise illuminates the East River skyline, the Brooklyn Bridge, and the South Street Seaport.

use letter rate

THIS AREA FOR OFFICIAL POSTAL USE ONLY

Photographs by JON ORTNER

The buildings of Central Park South provide a sharp contrast to the lush green and tranquility of Sheep Meadow in Central Park.

use
letter
rate

THIS AREA FOR OFFICIAL POSTAL USE ONLY

Photographs by
JON ORTNER

NEW YORK

The Plaza Hotel sits at the southeastern edge of Central Park. The Gapstow Bridge is shown in this winter scene.

use letter rate

THIS AREA FOR OFFICIAL POSTAL USE ONLY

Photographs by
JON ORTNER

The Metropolitan Opera House is the centerpiece of Lincoln Center for the Performing Arts on the Upper West Side of Manhattan.

use
letter
rate

THIS AREA FOR OFFICIAL POSTAL USE ONLY

Photographs by
JON ORTNER

ONE WAY

NEW YORK

Rush hour traffic on Park Avenue moves south to pass under the Helmsley and Met Life Buildings.

use
letter
rate

THIS AREA FOR OFFICIAL POSTAL USE ONLY

Photographs by
JON ORTNER

A statue of Atlas stands before the dramatic rise of the 850-foot RCA Building that identifies Rockefeller Center.

use
letter
rate

THIS AREA FOR OFFICIAL POSTAL USE ONLY

Photographs by
JON ORTNER

Famous Name
Men's
Clothing and
Furnishings
Usually
Below
Original
Wholesale!

NEW YORK

Built in 1902, the Flatiron Building is one of the earliest examples of a steel frame building. Located where Fifth Avenue and Broadway intersect at 23rd Street, it has become one of the most popular and photographed skyscrapers in New York City.

use
letter
rate

THIS AREA FOR OFFICIAL POSTAL USE ONLY

Photographs by
JON ORTNER

NEW YORK The World Financial Center and the Woolworth Building are dwarfed by the 110-story towers of the World Trade Center.

use
letter
rate

#43658 © Impact

THIS AREA FOR OFFICIAL POSTAL USE ONLY

Photographs by
JON ORTNER

HER IN EVE Y ART BROU
TO MORTAL A MEANS T

Since the 1930's, the gold-leaf statue of Prometheus has presided over ice skaters in winter and outdoor diners in warm months in the heart of Rockefeller Center.

use
letter
rate

THIS AREA FOR OFFICIAL POSTAL USE ONLY

Photographs by
JON ORTNER

RADIO CITY MUSIC HALL
RADIO CITY MUSIC HALL
Music Hall RADIO CITY Music Hall RADIO CITY
THE GREATEST STARS ON THE GREAT STAGE
THE GREATEST STARS ON THE GREAT STAGE

NEW
YORK

Radio City Music Hall –"The Greatest Stars on the Great Stage." This world famous New York City landmark is located at 50th Street and Sixth Avenue at Rockefeller Center. Home of the Rockettes, Radio City hosts spectacular Christmas and Easter shows, along with famous stars year-round.

use
letter
rate

THIS AREA FOR OFFICIAL POSTAL USE ONLY

Photographs by
JON ORTNER

STREET
BUSES AND TAXIS
Tickets
Information

NEW YORK

Grand Central Station is located beneath the Met Life Building at 42nd Street and Park Avenue.

use
letter
rate

THIS AREA FOR OFFICIAL POSTAL USE ONLY

Photographs by
JON ORTNER

NEW YORK

The Statue of Liberty raises her torch in front of the World Trade Center–the tallest buildings in New York City at 110 stories each.

use
letter
rate

THIS AREA FOR OFFICIAL POSTAL USE ONLY

Photographs by
JON ORTNER

NEW YORK

The buildings of Central Park West provide a sharp contrast to the autumn colors and tranquility of Central Park.

use letter rate

THIS AREA FOR OFFICIAL POSTAL USE ONLY

Photographs by
JON ORTNER

NEW YORK

Seen from the Brooklyn Bridge, the setting sun and brilliant glow of city lights are reflected in the East River.

use
letter
rate

THIS AREA FOR OFFICIAL POSTAL USE ONLY

Photographs by
JON ORTNER

NEW YORK The statue of Mercury above Grand Central Station provides a sharp contrast to the architecture of the Chrysler Building.

use
letter
rate

THIS AREA FOR OFFICIAL POSTAL USE ONLY

Photographs by
JON ORTNER

NEW YORK The American Museum of Natural History houses many collections and exhibitions enough to satisfy a variety of tastes.

use letter rate

#43666 © Impact

THIS AREA FOR OFFICIAL POSTAL USE ONLY

Photographs by JON ORTNER

NEW YORK

Fireworks over the Brooklyn Bridge illuminate the sky. Completed in 1883, the Brooklyn Bridge was designed by John Roebling, a German immigrant, and engineered by his son Washington.

use letter rate

THIS AREA FOR OFFICIAL POSTAL USE ONLY

Photographs by
JON ORTNER

NEW YORK

When completed in 1930, the art deco Chrysler Building was the tallest in the world at 1046 feet. The Empire State Building was completed in 1931 and stands 306.8 feet tall; although no longer the tallest, it is probably the most famous.

use
letter
rate

THIS AREA FOR OFFICIAL POSTAL USE ONLY

Photographs by
JON ORTNER